Music
from Our Lord's
Holy Heaven

Music from Our Lord's Holy Heaven

GATHERED AND SUNG BY GLORIA JEAN PINKNEY

ART BY JERRY PINKNEY,

BRIAN PINKNEY,

AND MYLES C. PINKNEY

PRELUDE BY TROY PINKNEY-RAGSDALE

HarperCollinsPublishers

Amistad

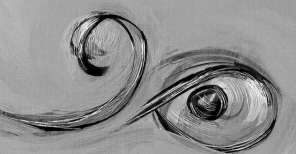

Contents

Music for the Heart

BY TROY PINKNEY-RAGSDALE

Music offers a magical space for children as well as adults. Within a song one can find warmth, motivation, and a chance to express oneself. As a child life specialist who's worked on the pediatric ward of an inner-city hospital, I've had the opportunity to witness the positive effects of all kinds of music.

Over the years I have come to realize that the inspiring words and rhythms of spirituals soothe, comfort, uplift, give joy, and promote healing. Long before youngsters learn the meaning of lyrics, they are aware of the effects inspirational music has on grown-ups. From as far back as I can remember, music has been a part of my life. Listening to the calming sound of my mother singing as my brothers and I got ready for Sunday School—even today that wonderful memory evokes powerful emotions.

Spirituals are so melodic that even a very young child can quickly hum a tune and often remember the words. There is nothing more pleasing than to see children as young as three lifting their voices during the devotional service at my church. We feel unified as a congregation when our children lead us in hymns of worship and praise.

Sharing inspirational songs with children is a unique way to teach the wonders of God, for singing lets them actively participate in the learning process. At many churches and religious schools, spirituals and hymns are an integral part of youth ministry performances. For example, in a black history play, my church used music to illustrate the journey of slaves from captivity to freedom.

Spirit-filled songs such as "Glory, Glory, Hallelujah!," "We Are Climbing Jacob's Ladder," "Go, Tell It on the Mountain," and "This Little Light of Mine" resonate from the heart to bring biblical stories and lessons to life. Music transcends the boundaries that divide us; we become one body, one spiritual family.

Adoration

Make a joyful noise unto the LORD, all ye lands. Serve the LORD
with gladness: come before His presence with singing.

PSALM 100:1–2

Old-Time Religion

Chorus:
Give me that old-time religion,
That old-time religion,
That old-time religion,
It's good enough for me.

Makes me love everybody,
Makes me love everybody.
Makes me love everybody.
It's good enough for me.

It will take us all to heaven,
It will take us all to heaven.
It will take us all to heaven.
It's good enough for me.

PSALM 9:1–2

I will praise Thee, O LORD, with my whole heart; I will show forth all Thy marvelous works. I will be glad and rejoice in Thee: I will sing praise to Thy name, O Thou Most High.

4

Holy, Holy, Holy

Holy, holy, holy! Lord God Almighty!
Early in the morning our song shall rise to Thee;
Holy, holy, holy, merciful and mighty!
God in three persons, blessed Trinity!

Holy, holy, holy! All the saints adore Thee,
Casting down their golden crowns around the glassy sea;
Cherubim and seraphim falling down before Thee,
Who was, and is, and evermore shall be.

Holy, holy, holy! Though the darkness hide Thee,
Though the eye of sinful man Thy glory may not see;
Only Thou art holy; there is none beside Thee,
Perfect in power, in love, in purity.

Holy, holy, holy! Lord God Almighty!
All Thy works shall praise Thy Name, in earth,
    and sky, and sea;
Holy, holy, holy; merciful and mighty!
God in three Persons, blessed Trinity!

PSALM 105:1–2

O give thanks unto the LORD; call upon His name: make known His deeds among the people. Sing unto Him, sing psalms unto Him: talk ye of all His wondrous works.

This Is My Father's World

This is my Father's world, and to my listening ears
All nature sings, and round me rings the music of the spheres.
This is my Father's world: I rest me in the thought
Of rocks and trees, of skies and seas;
His hand the wonders wrought.

This is my Father's world, the birds their carols raise,
The morning light, the lily white, declare their Maker's praise.
This is my Father's world: He shines in all that's fair;
In the rustling grass I hear Him pass;
He speaks to me everywhere.

This is my Father's world, dreaming, I see His face.
I open my eyes, and in glad surprise cry, "The Lord is in this place."
This is my Father's world, from the shining courts above,
The Beloved One, His Only Son,
Came—a pledge of deathless love.

PSALM 148:5

Let them praise the name of the LORD: for He commanded,
and they were created.

Glory, Glory, Hallelujah!

Chorus:
Glory, glory, hallelujah!
Since I laid my burden down,
Glory, glory, hallelujah!
Since I laid my burden down.

I feel better, so much better,
Since I laid my burden down,
I feel better, so much better,
Since I laid my burden down.

Feel like shouting "Hallelujah!"
Since I laid my burden down,
Feel like shouting "Hallelujah!"
Since I laid my burden down.

I'm going home to be with Jesus,
Since I laid my burden down,
I'm going home to be with Jesus,
Since I laid my burden down.

PSALM 89:1

I will sing of the mercies of the LORD for ever: with my mouth will I make known Thy faithfulness to all generations.

8

Praise Him, All Ye Little Children

Praise Him, praise Him, all ye little children,
God is love, God is love;
Praise Him, praise Him, all ye little children,
God is love, God is love.

Love Him, love Him, all ye little children,
God is love, God is love;
Love Him, love Him, all ye little children,
God is love, God is love.

Thank Him, thank Him, all ye little children,
God is love, God is love;
Thank Him, thank Him, all ye little children,
God is love, God is love.

PSALM 150:1–2

Praise ye the LORD. Praise God in His sanctuary: praise Him in the firmament of His power. Praise Him for His mighty acts; praise Him according to His excellent greatness.

Every Time I Feel the Spirit

Chorus:
Every time I feel the Spirit
Moving in my heart,
I will pray.
Every time I feel the Spirit
Moving in my heart,
I will pray.

Up on the mountain my Lord spoke,
Out of His mouth came fire and smoke.
In the valley, on my knees,
Ask my Lord have mercy, please.

Jordan River chilly and cold,
Chill the body but not the soul.
All around me look so fine,
Ask my Lord if all was mine.

Ain't but one train runs this track,
It runs to heaven and runs right back.
Saint Peter waiting at the gate,
Says, "Come on, sinner, don't be late."

PSALM 55:17

Evening, and morning, and at noon, will I pray, and cry aloud:
and He shall hear my voice.

Come by Here, My Lord

Come by here, my Lord, Kuumbya!
Come by here, my Lord, Kuumbya!
Come by here, my Lord, Kuumbya!
O Lord, Kuumbya

Someone's crying, Lord, Kuumbya!
Someone's crying, Lord, Kuumbya!
Someone's crying, Lord, Kuumbya!
O Lord, Kuumbya

Someone's singing, Lord, Kuumbya!
Someone's singing, Lord, Kuumbya!
Someone's singing, Lord, Kuumbya!
O Lord, Kuumbya

Someone's praying, Lord, Kuumbya!
Someone's praying, Lord, Kuumbya!
Someone's praying, Lord, Kuumbya!
O Lord, Kuumbya

Someone needs you, Lord, Kuumbya!
Someone needs you, Lord, Kuumbya!
Someone needs you, Lord, Kuumbya!
O Lord, Kuumbya

PSALM 51:10–12

Create in me a clean heart, O God; and renew a right spirit within me. Cast me not away from Thy presence; and take not Thy Holy Spirit from me. Restore unto me the joy of Thy salvation; and uphold me with Thy free Spirit.

Spiritual Wayfarers

Cause me to hear Thy loving-kindness in the morning; for in
Thee do I trust: cause me to know the way wherein I should
walk; for I lift up my soul unto Thee.

PSALM 143:8

Wade in the Water

Chorus:
Wade in the water.
Wade in the water, children.
Wade in the water.
God's gonna trouble the water.

Well, who are these children all dressed in red?
God's gonna trouble the water.
Must be the children that Moses led.
God's gonna trouble the water.

Who's that young girl dressed in white?
God's gonna trouble the water.
Must be the children of Israelites.
God's gonna trouble the water.

Jordan's water is chilly and cold.
God's gonna trouble the water.
Chills the body, but not the soul.
God's gonna trouble the water.

If you get there before I do.
God's gonna trouble the water.
Tell all of my friends I'm coming too.
God's gonna trouble the water.

PSALM 118:14

The LORD is my strength and song, and is become my salvation.

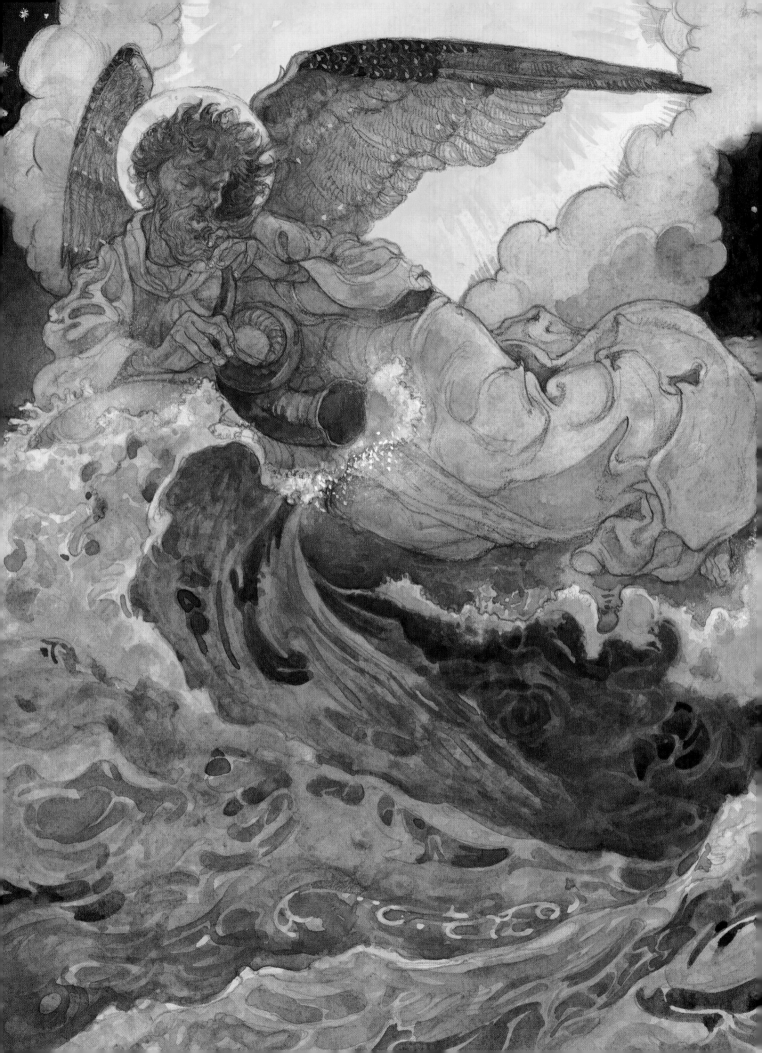

Go Down, Moses

When Israel was in Egypt's land,
Let my people go,
Oppressed so hard they could not stand,
Let my people go.

The Lord told Moses what to do,
Let my people go,
To lead the Hebrew children through,
Let my people go.

As Israel stood by the waterside,
Let my people go,
At God's command it did divide,
Let my people go.

Pharaoh said that he'd go across,
Let my people go,
But Pharaoh and his host were lost,
Let my people go.

Chorus:
Go down, Moses,
Way down in Egypt's land.
Tell old Pharaoh
Let my people go.

PSALM 105:26–27

He sent Moses His servant; and Aaron whom He had chosen.
They showed His signs among them, and wonders in the land
of Ham.

Joshua Fit the Battle of Jericho

Chorus:
Joshua fit the battle of Jericho,
Jericho, Jericho;
Joshua fit the battle of Jericho
And the walls came tumbling down.

You may talk about your kings of Gideon,
You may talk about your men of Saul,
But there's none like good old Joshua
At the battle of Jericho.

Now the Lord commanded Joshua:
"I command you and obey you must;
You just march straight to those city walls
And the walls will turn to dust."

Straight up to the walls of Jericho
He marched with spear in hand;
"Go blow that ram's horn," Joshua cried,
"For the battle is in my hand."

The lamb ram sheep horns began to blow,
And the trumpets began to sound,
And Joshua commanded, "Now children, shout!"
And the walls came tumbling down.

PSALM 140:6–7

I said unto the LORD, Thou art my God: hear the voice of my supplications, O LORD. O GOD the LORD, the strength of my salvation, Thou hast covered my head in the day of battle.

We Are Climbing Jacob's Ladder

We are climbing Jacob's ladder,
We are climbing Jacob's ladder,
We are climbing Jacob's ladder,
Soldiers of the cross.

Every round goes higher, higher,
Every round goes higher, higher,
Every round goes higher, higher,
Soldiers of the cross.

Sinner, do you love my Jesus?
Sinner, do you love my Jesus?
Sinner, do you love my Jesus?
Soldiers of the cross.

If you love Him, why not serve Him?
If you love Him, why not serve Him?
If you love Him, why not serve Him?
Soldiers of the cross.

PSALM 46:10–11

Be still, and know that I am God: I will be exalted among the heathen, I will be exalted in the earth. The LORD of hosts is with us; the God of Jacob is our refuge.

The Angels Are Watching over Me

All night, all day,
The angels keep a'watching over me, my Lord.
All night, all day,
The angels keep watching over me.

Someday Peter and someday Paul,
The angels are watching over me—
Ain't but one God made us all,
The angels are watching over me.

You get there before I do,
The angels are watching over me—
Tell all my friends I'm coming too.
The angels are watching over me.

PSALM 91:4–5

He shall cover thee with His feathers, and under His wings shalt
thou trust: His truth shall be thy shield and buckler. Thou shalt not
be afraid for the terror by night; nor for the arrow that flieth by day.

Walk in Jerusalem Just like John

Chorus:
I want to be ready,
I want to be ready,
I want to be ready
To walk in Jerusalem just like John.

John said the city was just four square,
Walk in Jerusalem just like John,
And he declared he'd meet me there,
Walk in Jerusalem just like John.

Oh, John, oh, John, what do you say,
Walk in Jerusalem just like John,
I'll be there in the coming day,
Walk in Jerusalem just like John.

PSALM 102:19–22

For He hath looked down from the height of His sanctuary; from heaven did the LORD behold the earth; To hear the groaning of the prisoner; to loose those that are appointed to death; To declare the name of the LORD in Zion, and His praise in Jerusalem; When the people are gathered together, and the kingdoms, to serve the LORD.

Oh! What a Beautiful City

Chorus:
Oh! what a beautiful city,
Oh! what a beautiful city,
Oh! what a beautiful city,
Twelve gates to the city, Hallelu!

Three gates in the east,
Three gates in the west,
Three gates in the north,
And three gates in the south,
Making it twelve gates to the city, Hallelu!

My Lord built that city,
Said it was just four square;
Wanted all you sinners
To meet Him in the air;
'Cause He built twelve gates to the city,
    Hallelu!

PSALM 24:9–10

Lift up your heads, O ye gates; even lift them up, ye everlasting doors; and the King of glory shall come in. Who is this King of glory? the LORD of hosts, He is the King of glory.

23

The Good Shepherd

The LORD is my shepherd; I shall not want. He maketh me to lie down in green pastures: He leadeth me beside the still waters.

PSALM 23:1–2

Go, Tell It on the Mountain

Chorus:
Go, tell it on the mountain, over the hills and everywhere,
Go, tell it on the mountain that Jesus Christ is born.

While shepherds kept their watching over silent flocks by night,
Behold throughout the heavens there shone a holy light.

The shepherds feared and trembled when lo! above the earth
Rang out the angel chorus that hailed our Savior's birth.

Down in a lowly manger the humble Christ was born,
And God sent us salvation that blessed Christmas morn.

PSALM 103:20

Bless the LORD, ye His angels, that excel in strength, that do His commandments, hearkening unto the voice of His word.

Tell Me the Stories of Jesus

Tell me the stories of Jesus I love to hear;
Things I would ask Him to tell me if He were here;
Scenes by the wayside, tales of the sea,
Stories of Jesus, tell them to me.

First let me hear how the children stood round His knee,
And I shall fancy His blessing resting on me;
Words full of kindness, deeds full of grace,
All in the love light of Jesus' face.

Into the city I'd follow the children's band,
Waving a branch of the palm tree high in my hand.
One of His heralds, yes, I would sing
Loudest hosannas, "Jesus is King!"

PSALM 8:3–4

When I consider Thy heavens, the work of Thy fingers, the moon and the stars, which Thou hast ordained; What is man, that Thou art mindful of him? And the son of man, that Thou visitest him?

Jesus Loves the Little Children

Jesus loves the little children,
All the children of the world.
Red and yellow, black and white,
All are precious in His sight,
Jesus loves the little children of the world.

Jesus died for all the children,
All the children of the world.
Red and yellow, black and white,
All are precious in His sight,
Jesus loves the little children of the world.

PSALM 127:3

Lo, children are a heritage of the LORD and the fruit of the womb is His reward.

Shine on Me

Chorus:
Shine on me,
Shine on me.
Let the light from the lighthouse shine on me.
O shine on me,
Shine on me.
Let the light from the lighthouse shine on me.

I heard the voice of Jesus say,
"Come unto me and rest;
Lay down, thou weary one, lay down
Thy head upon my breast."

With pitying eyes the Prince of Peace
Beheld our helpless grief;
He saw, and O amazing love!
He came to our relief.

PSALM 89:15–16

Blessed is the people that know the joyful sound: they shall walk,
O LORD, in the light of Thy countenance. In Thy name shall they
rejoice all the day: and in Thy righteousness shall they be exalted.

Lead, Kindly Light

Lead, kindly Light,
Amid the encircling gloom,
Lead Thou me on;
The night is dark,
And I am far from home;
Lead Thou me on!
Keep Thou my feet;
I do not ask to see
The distant scene:
One step enough for me.

PSALM 18:28

For Thou wilt light my candle: the LORD my God will enlighten
my darkness.

He's Got the Whole World in His Hands

He's got the whole world in His hands,
He's got the big, round world in His hands,
He's got the whole world in His hands,
He's got the whole world in His hands.

He's got the flowers and the trees in His hands,
He's got the flowers and the trees in His hands,
He's got the flowers and the trees in His hands,
He's got the whole world in His hands.

He's got the little bitty baby in His hands,
He's got the little bitty baby in His hands,
He's got the little bitty baby in His hands,
He's got the whole world in His hands.

He's got you and me, sister, in His hands,
He's got you and me, sister, in His hands,
He's got you and me, sister, in His hands,
He's got the whole world in His hands.

He's got you and me, brother, in His hands,
He's got you and me, brother, in His hands,
He's got you and me, brother, in His hands,
He's got the whole world in His hands.

PSALM 19:11

The heavens declare the glory of God; and the firmament showeth His handiwork.

Christ the Lord Is Risen Today

Christ, the Lord, is risen today, *Alleluia!*
Sons of men and angels say, *Alleluia!*
Raise your joys and triumphs high, *Alleluia!*
Sing, ye heavens, and, earth, reply, *Alleluia!*

Risen with Him, we upward move, *Alleluia!*
Still we seek the things above, *Alleluia!*
Still pursue and kiss the Son, *Alleluia!*
Seated on His Father's throne, *Alleluia!*

King of glory, soul of bliss, *Alleluia!*
Everlasting life is this, *Alleluia!*
Thee to know, Thy power to prove, *Alleluia!*
Thus to sing, and thus to love, *Alleluia!*

PSALM 16:11

Thou wilt show me the path of life: in Thy presence is fullness of joy;
at Thy right hand there are pleasures for evermore.

This Little Light of Mine

Chorus:
This little light of mine, I'm gonna let it shine;
This little light of mine, I'm gonna let it shine;
This little light of mine, I'm gonna let it shine;
Let it shine, let it shine, let it shine.

God gave me a little light, I'm gonna let it shine;
God gave me a little light, I'm gonna let it shine;
God gave me a little light, I'm gonna let it shine;
Let it shine, let it shine, let it shine.

Won't let Satan blow it out, I'm gonna let it shine;
Won't let Satan blow it out, I'm gonna let it shine;
Won't let Satan blow it out, I'm gonna let it shine;
Let it shine, let it shine, let it shine.

Let it shine till Jesus comes, I'm gonna let it shine;
Let it shine till Jesus comes, I'm gonna let it shine;
Let it shine till Jesus comes, I'm gonna let it shine;
Let it shine, let it shine, let it shine.

PSALM 119:105

Thy word is a lamp unto my feet, and a light unto my path.

Jerry

Gloria

My mother

Great-aunt Alma

Our prom

Our wedding

Scott and Myles

Myles

Troy

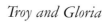

Troy and Gloria

Brian

Brian and Jerry

Clockwise: Myles, Jerry, Scott, Brian, Troy, Gloria

Melodious Journey

BY GLORIA JEAN PINKNEY

When I was a child growing up in my great-aunt Alma Cannon's home in Philadelphia, Pennsylvania, I'd often spend after-school time singing as loud as I could manage. My aunt, who worked long hours to make a living, owned a three-story brick house. It had excellent acoustics. She also had an upright piano, so I taught myself to play by ear. Singing spirited songs never failed to bring comfort to my hours alone. My piano chords filled the empty rooms of that row house with the sound of their lovely phrases. My voice and the piano music brought to mind the time I had spent listening to my mother Ernestine's beautiful, southern way of singing. She passed away when I was eight years old. My mother would often sing down-home spirituals that she had learned at the Hilly Branch Church in North Carolina. These are cherished memories. I liked spirituals then. Today I'm in love with them.

Aunt Alma was a Christian. "Hurry up," she exclaimed most Sunday mornings. "We don't want to miss the choir marching in!" Long hours in Emmanuel Institutional Baptist Church were okay with me because of the Gospel Choir. I was fascinated by their uplifting songs and ever-swaying robes. Plus our pastor had an exceptional singing voice. Afterward I would long for Mondays so that I could practice. Those private concerts were often filled with songs that I had heard the day before.

Another fond memory is of Sunday evenings spent lying in the twin bed next to my aunt's listening to radio ministries. A favorite program came from a singing preacher named Prophet Cherry. Memories of his haunting, poetic style, intertwined with the sounds of his harmonica, cause me to long for another opportunity to hear him. His music ministry, sung in broken English, was often difficult to understand. Yet we were always able to feel the Spirit within his words. Aunt Alma called it "ole timey down home singing."

My aunt was a no-nonsense person who preferred listening to three types of music: religious, country and western, and classical orchestra (if the orchestra was directed by Paul Whiteman). Aunt Alma's day off was usually Saturday. We spent most of it doing housework, but when our chores were finished it was time for bonding. Favorite pastimes were singing songs from the *Baptist Hymnal* and watching the Grand Ole Opry. That show always ended with a spiritual. Every now and then, when my cousins Bubby and Sissie were over, the three of us would put on a talent show for Aunt Alma. I can still picture myself centered in front of the parlor mantelpiece attempting to sound like a favorite gospel singer.

Once The Dixie Hummingbirds, The Five Blind Boys, and the Soul Stirrers gave a concert at Emmanuel. They came with all kinds of amplified instruments. That night I became an admirer of harmonization. Then, when our pastor befriended Miss Mahalia Jackson, I was blessed to experience her extraordinary voice and her love of gospel music from an up-front pew.

In my young years I dreamed of becoming a professional singer. Somewhere along the way my plan changed. So I sang for my husband and our children. Music is an integral part of the Pinkney household. When our children were babies, I'd often sing them to sleep. When they were in grade school, we had a piano and, for a short time, a pump organ. I taught all who were interested the tunes that I knew, which included spirituals and boogie-woogie.

When our four children became teenagers, they joined the Youth Choir at church, and the glee club, orchestra, and band at school. Two of our boys played the drums at church and school. All of them studied at least one instrument and have pleasant singing voices. Music has always been part of our home, whether coming from their practicing, my voice, or our all-inclusive collection of records, tapes, and CDs. When reminiscing, my children recall lying in bed listening to melodies traveling up the open stairwell. Today I continue to sing while folding laundry or when paying bills.

A spirited song never ceases to make laborious things feel easier. Oftentimes, in my young years, I was called upon to sing solos in elementary school as well as at church. Performing in front of a large crowd was a traumatic experience. I can vividly recall trembling through verse after verse of my first solo in elementary school, "Mockingbird Hill." Then the same fear surfaced at church. I believe I was around ten years old. The song was "My Hope Is Built on Nothing Less." On both occasions an unrecognizable voice came out of my mouth. I didn't know then that all I had to do was pray, "Lord, help me," and believe the comforting words that I was singing about Jesus. Many decades would pass before I made this request, "Lord, give me courage to sing in public." I'm happy to say our Lord answered. Today I'm often a soloist at our church. Also, most of my author presentations open with a spiritual journey song. Music, especially songs of faith, lifts my inner being and warms the hearts of audiences.

The opening selection, "Old-Time Religion," brings to mind *A Man Called Peter,* a religious movie I watched over and over as a child. I'll forever cherish the scene in which a group of young and older people sing this favorite. The last song, "This Little Light of Mine," causes me to think of a very special Elder who once graced our church. Mother Lucas would regularly light up the sanctuary with this song and a little Holy dance.

May the songs and scriptures chosen for *Music from Our Lord's Holy Heaven* serve to open your life ever wider to a faith-filled fellowship with the Holy One. These poetic, meaningful lyrics tell of our one God in three Persons: Father, Son, and Holy Spirit. They portray love, joy, hope, survival, heaven, salvation, and other goodly things. God bless you with His presence as you partake of these selections.

TO THE GLORY OF GOD AND ALL HIS CHILDREN
—The Pinkney Family

Amistad is an imprint of HarperCollins Publishers Inc.

Music from Our Lord's Holy Heaven
Compilation copyright © 2005 by Gloria Jean Pinkney
Illustrations copyright © 2005 by Jerry Pinkney, Brian Pinkney, and Myles C. Pinkney
Introduction copyright © 2005 by Troy Pinkney-Ragsdale
Manufactured in China. All rights reserved.
www.harperchildrens.com
Library of Congress Cataloging-in-Publication Data
Pinkney, Gloria Jean.
Music from our Lord's holy heaven / gathered and sung by Gloria Jean Pinkney ; art by
Jerry Pinkney, Brian Pinkney, and Myles C. Pinkney ; prelude by Troy Pinkney-Ragsdale.
p.   cm.
Contents: Music for the heart / by Troy Pinkney-Ragsdale — Adoration. Old-time religion ;
Holy, holy, holy ; This is my Father's world ; Glory, glory, hallelujah! ; Praise Him, all ye little children ;
Every time I feel the spirit ; Come by here, my Lord — Spiritual wayfarers. Wade in the water ; Go down, Moses ;
Joshua fit the battle of Jericho ; We are climbing Jacob's ladder ; The angels are watching over me ;
Walk in Jerusalem just like John ; Oh, what a beautiful city — The good shepherd.
Go, tell it on the mountain ; Tell me the stories of Jesus ; Jesus loves the little children ; Shine on me ;
Lead, kindly light ; He's got the whole world in his hands ; Christ the Lord is risen today ; This little light of mine —
Melodious journey / by Gloria Jean Pinkney.
ISBN 0-06-000768-0 — ISBN 0-06-000769-9 (lib. bdg.)
1. Hymns, English—Juvenile literature.   {1. Hymns.   2. Spirituals (Songs)}   I. Pinkney, Jerry, ill.
II. Pinkney, J. Brian, ill.   III. Pinkney, Myles C., ill.   IV. Title.
BV353 .P56   2005   264'.23—dc21   2002018939
Typography by Stephanie Bart-Horvath   1 2 3 4 5 6 7 8 9 10   ❖   First Edition